Cold Cases True Crime

True Murder Stories And Accounts Of Incredible Murder Mysteries From The Last Century

Brody Clayton

© **Copyright 2015 by Brody Clayton - All rights reserved.**

This document is geared towards providing exact and reliable information in regards to the topic and issue covered. The publication is sold with the idea that the publisher is not required to render accounting, officially permitted, or otherwise, qualified services. If advice is necessary, legal or professional, a practiced individual in the profession should be ordered.

- From a Declaration of Principles which was accepted and approved equally by a Committee of the American Bar Association and a Committee of Publishers and Associations.

In no way is it legal to reproduce, duplicate, or transmit any part of this document in either electronic means or in printed format. Recording of this publication is strictly prohibited and any storage of this document is not allowed unless with written permission from the publisher. All rights reserved.

The information provided herein is stated to be truthful

and consistent, in that any liability, in terms of inattention or otherwise, by any usage or abuse of any policies, processes, or directions contained within is the solitary and utter responsibility of the recipient reader. Under no circumstances will any legal responsibility or blame be held against the publisher for any reparation, damages, or monetary loss due to the information herein, either directly or indirectly.

Respective authors own all copyrights not held by the publisher.

The information herein is offered for informational purposes solely, and is universal as so. The presentation of the information is without contract or any type of guarantee assurance.

The trademarks that are used are without any consent, and the publication of the trademark is without permission or backing by the trademark owner. All trademarks and brands within this book are for clarifying purposes only and are the owned by the owners themselves, not affiliated with this document.

Brody Clayton

Cover image courtesy of Flickr - https://www.flickr.com/photos/zionfiction/9568000446/

Cold Cases True Crime

Table of Contents

Introduction	vii
Chapter 1: Hell Hath No Fury Than A Woman Scorned	1
Chapter 2: What's in "C," "W," and "M"?	14
Chapter 3: Yours Truly, Anonymous	22
Chapter 4: When on Highway 16	31
Chapter 5: The Cannibal of Ziebice	42
Chapter 6: Hunting Children – The Family Business	52
Chapter 7: The High Priestess of Blood	61
Conclusion	75
Check Out My Other Books	76

Brody Clayton

Like FREE books?

Would you like them delivered to you every week?

Do you like non-fiction books on a huge range of different topics?

We send out FREE e-books every week so we can share our books with the world!

We have FREE books every week on AMAZON that we send to our email list.

So if you want in, then visit the link at the end of this book to sign up and sit back and wait for new books to be sent straight to your inbox!

Introduction

I want to thank you and congratulate you for purchasing the book, *"Cold Cases True Crime: True Murder Stories And Accounts Of Incredible Murder Mysteries From The Last Century"*.

Imagine if you had to wait decades for a crime to be solved: when the murderers are already dead and when the victim's loved ones have already lost so much, will there still be satisfaction?

This book will feature 7 cold cases, some of which are solved while the others still perplex the minds of not just the police and the families, but also those who are familiar with the events.

Thanks again, I hope you enjoy it!

Chapter 1:

Hell Hath No Fury Than A Woman Scorned

Sherri Rasmussen's case is one of the many testaments that no matter how cold a case could get, it can still be resolved. The story of her death involved a despicable feeling of jealousy from a woman scorned by an unrequited love.

John Ruetten was a charming man, those who remembered him described him as model-handsome, talkative, athletic, and intelligent. His dreams were big and his life was set in a solid direction, although he was still an undergraduate in UCLA, it was clear that he would go far. In many women's eyes before, John was perfection personified.

In his stay at the university, he met Stephanie Lazarus, a Political Science major in Simi Valley. Their friendship blossomed into something more akin to romantic intimacy as they discovered that they had a lot of things in common, for one, both were athletic.

Stephanie's thinking that they could be something more strengthened when John kept on allowing her to steal his shirts and take naked photographs of him as he slept. Finally, the two started to have a sexual relationship: from time to time, they met to sleep together.

In John's eyes, all those intimate moments were nothing but "necking" and "fooling around", but for Stephanie, they were quite serious.

Those serious feelings were further reinforced when they continued their sexual relationship even after graduation. By then, John was already employed in *Micropolis*, a hardware manufacturing company, and Stephanie entered the police academy.

In 1983, she was already a uniformed officer in the LAPD. At this point, the two still had different views of their relationship- while John was just playing around, Stephanie had already fallen deeply in love, though she didn't dare reveal her feelings.

In the summer of 1984, John met the woman of his dreams, Sherri Rasmussen. Like John, Sherri was also strong-willed and directed: she entered college when she was just 16 and after she graduated from *Loma Linda University*, she immediately became the nursing director of *Glendale Adventist Medical Center*, where one of her duties was to give lectures.

By all accounts, Sherri was the "hot stuff"-- all the things

John wanted in a girl, when the two met each other, nothing else seemed to matter because they were instantly in love. In November of 1985, the two got married.

On February 24, 1986, just a few months after John and Sherri exchanged wedding vows, they fell into the comforts of their new life. On that day, John woke up early, eager to work at his new job in an engineering company. Sherri on the other hand, did not feel like working: she was supposed to handle a class of nursing students, but was more inclined to call in sick.

John encouraged his wife to go to the class and just get it over with, but when he left their Van Nuys condominium at 7:20 am, Sherri was still ambivalent on what to do.

Since he knew it was still early, John opted to drop some clothes off to the laundry shop before heading to his office. It was a good choice because he still arrived at work shortly before 8:00 am, he wanted to call Sherri, but decided against it just in case she chose to stay home and sleep.

After a few hours, he finally called home, and when no one answered, he assumed that his wife attended the class after all, so he phoned her office. Sherri's secretary answered and told him that she still had not seen his wife, but she assured John that it was normal.

Apparently, during Mondays, Sherri often went straight to class. John let it go for a while, but he tried calling home again 3 more times throughout the day, however, all attempts to reach Sherri were futile. At this point, John was still not worried, but he thought it was odd for Sherri not to activate the answering machine, "Sometimes, she forgets", John reasoned.

Still unconcerned about his wife, John left his office, went to the laundry shop to pick up the clean clothes, and went to a UPS store. When he got home, he noticed several things which were not in order in their Van Nuys home.

For a start, the door at the garage was drawn up, and then on the floor, were shards of glass. Sherri's car was also nowhere in sight, but he assumed that the shards of glass were from her car's window. Thinking that his wife only had small troubles (very common, according to him), he picked up the bags of laundry, went upstairs to their living room, and stopped dead. The inner door to their living room was not just unlocked, it was slightly ajar. When he entered, he was greeted with Sherri's lifeless body.

As his mind refused to believe what was happening, he assumed that Sherri was just asleep-- maybe she took a fall and lost consciousness. No problem, he just had to shake her a little to wake her up. But upon closer look, he knew something more terrible than falling happened.

Sherri was on her back, still in her night robe, which was slightly open. Sherri appeared to be assaulted: her face was swollen and bloody, and the look on her eyes depicted shock, it was a frozen picture of her reaction to whatever transpired before her death.

Both of her hands were raised, slightly bent and one of her legs was bent at the knee, as if she tried to get up, but couldn't. John dared to touch her left leg and felt it was cold, he also palpated for a pulse on her wrist, but he found none.

As if his mind still couldn't accept the idea that their blooming marriage life was cut short, he inspected his wife's face a bit more and learned that the blood was dry. Her right eye, battered and blue, was closed, unlike her left, which was slightly open, staring in shock and as if she managed to draw one final tortured gasp, her mouth was opened a little. Finally, John called 911 after seeing that at the right center of Sherri's chest, was a bullet hole.

When the authorities arrived, they didn't just focus on Sherri's body, so some things became clearer. For instance, a fight happened, possibly when Sherri struggled to save herself. The two display shelves were misaligned, an amplifier and receiver were dangling on top of the television, the tall stereo was knocked over and it dropped near Sherri's head (its wires were missing), and a vase was also broken with its shards on the floor.

From there, the police went to the stairs leading to the second floor, and in the room, they saw that the VCR and CD player were neatly stacked, as if someone was bringing them, but had forgotten to. It was a bloody scene, to say the least, because on top of the CD player, the police found a smear of blood, and when they checked the east wall and the front door, smears of blood were also present.

On the floor near the front door, two intertwined cords were found, and they found it to be the missing cords of the stereo. Upstairs, one of the two door glasses on the balcony was shattered-- their shards were the ones John had seen at the garage. Other than these things, there was no sign of forced entry, and when they inspected, nothing seemed to be missing.

Whoever the murderer was, he or she didn't come to steal, and Sherri probably opened up the door for him or her.

Homicide detective Lyle Meyer discovered another clue: there, sitting in the living room chair, was a pink and green quilted blanket with a bullet hole and powder burns. When he cross matched it with the bullet holes found in Sherri's body, he deduced that the victim had been shot three times.

The first was fired from a distance, and then the next two were shot point blank against Sherri's chest; the blanket was used to muffle the sounds. Although there were three shots, only two of the .38 caliber bullets were recovered, which made the police conclude that one of the bullets passed through her chest.

Someone really wanted her dead, for only one shot was enough to kill her, and yet the perpetrator chose to "polish" the act by firing twice more. The condition of Sherri's face, swollen, battered, and bloody, was a testament of anger. In her inner left forearm, a bite mark was discovered; the police took samples of the saliva for DNA and a cast was created out of the bite mark for a tooth comparison.

Sherri's car was found a week later on the streets near Van Nuys, its door was unlocked, a blood spot and a strand of brown hair were found.

But despite all the evidence leading to the conclusion that whoever killed Sherri had a personal vendetta against her, detective Meyer only suggested that burglars entered their home, that they panicked when they saw her, and in their desperation to escape, they killed her.

He drew this conclusion after finding out from the neighbors that two unidentified men were ransacking houses in the area and at one point, they hurt a woman. John was not appeased by this knowledge-- why didn't they just run? Why was there a need to hurt his wife when she was clearly unarmed and defenseless? Why did they shoot her three times?

Nels Rasmussen, Sherri's father, was informed about Sherri's death a day later by John's father. He was furious, to say the least, for if his beloved daughter had died the day before, then why was he only being informed now? He wanted to speak to John directly, but since John's father sensed his hostility, he refused: he didn't want to subject his son to any more stress.

Stricken with grief from losing his daughter, Nels spent the whole night thinking back and gathering as much information as he could recall about his daughter's situation. From there, he formed a suspicion on who killed his daughter, and he made his idea known to the police.

"Did you check on John's ex-girlfriend, the ex-cop?" he told the police. Apparently, Sherri had been confiding with Nels about this woman who couldn't seem to accept the fact that John was taken. A few weeks before the wedding, the said woman showed up unannounced at their home with a pair of water skis she wanted John to wax.

Sherri told her father that she knew the skis were just mere excuses for the woman to intrude their home, but John still waxed the skis despite her objections. Instead of standing up for her, John merely assured her that all was over between the two of them, that she was just a dorm pal, and that the thing they had was not even serious to begin with.

Said woman returned again to take the skis, but this time, Sherri asked her to leave as soon as the the skis were in her hands. It turned out that the woman was persistent. For she still met John for lunch, and even had the nerve to go to Glendale where Sherri worked.

Yes, that woman was Stephanie Lazarus.

Nels recounted everything to the police, but detective Meyer dismissed his suspicions and even claimed that "he watched too many cop shows on TV". For Detective Meyer, only two things could have happened: either John killed Sherri, or some house intruders did.

Since he felt John's grief to be genuine, and that there was no reason for him to kill his wife, he disregarded the idea that John was the killer, in fact, he even assured John that he was not a suspect.

When he asked John about Nels' suspicion that Stephanie was the murderer, John shrugged it off, saying that it couldn't be that. Detective Meyer, who was obviously thinking only on the surface of the box, believed him.

Nels didn't find peace; the idea that some burglars killed his daughter didn't make sense to him. One, the house was a mess, and it seemed like a fight went on for almost an hour, how could Sherri fight two men for that long?

Also, the bite mark on her forearm was an indication that the suspect was a woman. All the records that mentioned Stephanie Lazarus' name were not included in Sherri's file, as if the police were protecting one of their own.

23 years later, Nels would be proven correct.

In 2001, Police Chief Bernard Parks created the LAPD Cold Case Homicide Unit to solve forgotten crimes systematically. Criminologist Jennifer Francis took one look at Sherri's case and noticed something strange.

Her file said that a swab was taken, but it was not included in the evidence presented, naturally, she thought that it was still in the freezer, so they combed the laboratory and found it. When they checked, they found the truth-- the DNA was from a woman. Did they re-open the case?

No, because it was possible that one of the burglars was female. Hence, the swab was sent to the freezer once more, and it stayed there for another 4 years before

Sherri's case surfaced again.

Jim Nuttal, a homicide detective, was literally surfing through books of cold cases when he came upon Sherri's murder. Like Jennifer Francis, he found it odd that Detective Meyer insisted on two men as the killers when the saliva clearly belonged to a woman.

So he bravely took the initiative to investigate again. His first question was who among the women in Sherri's life would have the motive to kill her? Checking the files, they found a very "misplaced" info that said "John Reutten confirmed Stephanie Lazarus, PO, was an ex-girlfriend."

Why was it the only mention of Stephanie's name? Why didn't the police investigate it further? Sure, it could be that she was innocent, but calls and interviews should still have been made to at least eliminate her as a suspect.

Jim Nuttal and his team visited John who had then remarried to another woman and asked him about Stephanie. He honestly confided that Stephanie was Nels' theory, but he didn't believe it, and he still would not believe it. They went to Nels next and though he was annoyed, he still shared his opinion that Stephanie was the culprit.

So, they took the next step, check Stephanie's DNA to see if it would match the one they had from the swab. They followed her on one of her trips and when she dined, they retrieved the cup and straw she used. When the results came, it turned out positive, the one who had bitten Sherri on the day she was killed was Stephanie Lazarus.

The police invited Stephanie for an interview in the pretext that they were just interviewing people from the cold case of Sherri Rasmussen. They talked and throughout the conversation, Stephanie was "hot and cold", sometimes she remembered and sometimes she didn't.

She admitted that John still called her even when he was already dating Sherri, and that she conversed with the victim to tell her that she should make John stop from still carrying it on with her. The detectives asked her if she had a confrontation with Sherri on the day she was killed, but Stephanie said she couldn't remember.

"If something violent happened, you know, the "other woman" kind of thing, don't you think you would remember it?", one of the detectives asked her. They did this to make sure because it was still possible that Stephanie had just had a row with Sherri and had bitten her, but she didn't kill her.

If she admitted to the bite, then the police would have investigated further. But she denied ever being in the house on the day the murder took place, an obvious lie, because the DNA was a concrete proof that she was there.

Stephanie was free to leave, but when she reached the hallway, she was arrested.

Stephanie Lazarus was convicted in 2012 and was sentenced to spend 27 years in prison. She would be eligible for parole in the year 2039.

Chapter 2:

What's in "C," "W," and "M"?

The Alphabet Murders, or most appropriately, the Double Initials Murders was so called because the first and last names of the victims, who were little girls, begin with the same letter. On top of that, their remains were discovered in towns which also had the same initial.

On November 16, 1971, Carmen Colon, 10 years old, was asked by her grandparents to retrieve a prescription at a drugstore in West Main Street just near their home in Brown Street in Rochester, New York.

She was last seen leaving the said pharmacy, but she never returned home. 2 days later, Carmen's body was found by two teenage boys who were innocently bicycling in the Steams Road of Riga, a small town near Chili. From the autopsy, Carmen was a clear victim of rape and strangulation, her neck exhibiting fingernail marks.

Carmen's death instilled fear in the minds of the parents, the police worked double time, sparing no effort in finding the heartless killer who shattered the comfort of the whole town.

Some drivers from Riga came forward and reported to have seen a semi-nude girl running at Interstate 490, just a mile east of Riga, with a blue car tailing her. Sad as it was, those were the only "clues" the police found on who killed Carmen.

17 months later, on April 2, 1973, Wanda Walkowicz, 11, was also murdered. Like Carmen, Wanda was also from Rochester, New York, and her death also involved sexual assault and strangulation (but this time, using a belt).

According to reports, Wanda left their home in Avenue D because her mother asked her to do some grocery shopping in Conkey Avenue. After purchasing items worth $8.52, Wanda left the store and never returned home.

It took a whole day for her body to be recovered in State Route 104, in Webster, a mere 7 miles away from Rochester. When witnesses came forward, they mentioned that Wanda was taken by someone driving a brown car, different from the blue car which tailed Carmen in Riga.

Carmen Colon in Chili, Wanda Walkowicz in Webster, the pattern was there, but one could still easily say that it was all a coincidence. It would take Michelle Maenza to confirm the suspicion about the presence of a Double

Initials serial killer.

Michelle, only 11 at the time of her murder, was also from Rochester. On November 26, 1973, just 6 months after Wanda was killed, Michelle was seen by her uncle at Goodman Plaza, and so he offered to take her home but the young girl refused the offer. Two days later, her body turned up in Macedon, 15 miles away from Rochester.

Witnesses stated that she was seen inside a car in a fast-food restaurant in Penfield, and a man with no distinguishing characteristics, walked towards her while carrying a bag of food. Autopsy reports on Michelle's body revealed that she ate hamburger before she died.

One man also came forward and told the police that he had seen a car near Route 350 in Walworth, inside the car was a young girl who resembled Michelle. The witness tried to offer help because the other party appeared to have a flat tire, but it was clear that the man with Michelle didn't want any assistance.

After Michelle, no more victims surfaced, but the case was far from solved. Aside from their double initials, all the victims came from poor, Catholic families, all of them were not faring well in school, and each body recovered had a strand of white hair from a cat.

The letters C, M, and W were also the 3rd, 13th, and 23rd

letters of the alphabet. They also theorized that since the order of the killings was **C**armen, **W**anda, and **M**ichelle, it was a clue about what the killer was telling them-- "Come with me."

From accounts, the victims were last seen in busy places, so how possible could it be that three girls were abducted and killed without anyone noticing? It seemed like the murders were highly organized, hundreds of people were questioned, and a lot of suspects were interrogated, but the police never went near the point of solving the case.

Dennis Termini, a local fireman, was never proclaimed as a suspect, but he was a "person of interest". The police drew this conclusion from his involvement in a teenage rape case, which he was served an arrest warrant with.

The police also believed that the fireman suit he always carried was used to attract the victims. Dennis, however, didn't get the chance to prove his innocence regarding the Double Initials murders since he killed himself after the police tried to arrest him for the teenage rape case.

With the technology available today that wasn't before, the police were able to eliminate Dennis Termini. The fireman's body was exhumed and they took a DNA sample to compare with that taken from one of the crime scenes, however it didn't match.

Miguel Colon, Carmen's uncle, also became a suspect, for he left Rochester immediately after the slaying. When the police checked his car, they found Carmen's doll, and when they looked further, it seemed like the car had been cleaned.

Miguel was of course questioned, but he was not charged with anything. In 1991, he became involved in a domestic dispute where he injured his wife and brother-in-law, when the police arrived at their home, he taunted them to shoot him, but he went ahead and did the honors himself.

After his death, the police asked his family if he ever hinted about the Alphabet Murders, or at least, with Carmen's death, but they insisted Miguel's innocence.

Other persons of interest were Kenneth Bianchi and his cousin, Angelo Buono who committed the Hillside Strangler murders. However, due to the lack of evidence, they were never charged about the Double Initials murders.

More than 40 years later, the mystery still lives on. The loved ones these children left, gained nothing but harsh memories from the day they disappeared and onwards. Rita Walcowicz, now DeCann, Wanda's little sister, still thinks of rainy Mondays as dark days.

According to her, Wanda was taken a day before she

turned 10 years old, and when Wanda's body was recovered, it was her birthday. The event was even made more tragic by the fact that before Wanda's death, their father also died of heart attack.

Stephen, Michelle's older brother, also related on how upset their uncle had been. In his thoughts, if he just insisted on bringing Michelle home when he'd seen her in Goodman Plaza, she would still be alive now.

But no one was sure, because if the serial killer was really set on choosing Michelle as his/her victim, then he/she would have found another opportune time.

Several years after the Alphabet Murders in New York ceased, another case of Double Initials Murders took place in California, but the targets were grown women who were prostitutes. The victims were Roxanne Roggasch, Pamela Parsons, Tracy Tafoya, and Carmen Colon (a different person from the young girl in Rochester).

Unlike the New York Alphabet Murders, the California murders were less planned to say the least because the victims had no other similarities except for the fact that they were all prostitutes. Their remains were also not recovered in places which bore their initials. The California Alphabet Murders were also solved when 77 year old Joseph Naso was arrested for the killings.

Many speculated that Joseph Naso was also the killer in the New York case, because he was a native of Rochester. He also worked as a professional photographer which gave him time and resources to travel back and forth to California and New York.

The "rape diaries" he kept which was used as evidence against him also contained a death of a girl in "Buffalo Woods", which could mean Upstate New York. In 2013, Joseph Naso was sentenced to death for the California murders, but no other evidence linked him to the Rochester killings, especially when his DNA did not match the one found in the New York crime scene.

This case has been featured in many documentary shows, and was even turned into a film in 2008, *The Alphabet Killer*. In the movie, the suspect turned out to be a math tutor who previously worked in the school where all the victims were attending. This idea was taken from the findings that all the girls were not doing well in school.

If there's one word you could use to describe the alphabet murders, it would be enduring. More than 4 decades later and the motives are still unclear. Why did he choose the initials C, W, and M? What was the connection to number "3"?

If you'll notice, he had three victims, whose initials were the 3rd, 23rd, and 13th letter in the alphabet. What was his problem with poor, Catholic families? Why did he choose little girls who were not doing well in school?

Although there were many similarities, the police were unable to find a connection between three victims that could point them to the direction of the serial killer.

Chapter 3:

Yours Truly, Anonymous

Unsolved Mysteries, a famous show which started airing in 1987, continue to feature many stories of unsolved cases from missing persons, murders, wanted fugitives, and paranormal phenomena. Each episode, featuring 4 to 5 real-life cases, is aimed on publicizing the stories so that witnesses could come forward and report what they knew.

The show was a roaring success; more than 100 families were reunited with their loved ones and many wanted felons were caught with the help of the show. There were also instances when wrongfully convicted people were cleared due to the show's dedication in finding the truth.

With the show's success and good intentions, it was only natural for the crew and staff to receive letters of admiration and gratitude. However, on December 1993, Unsolved Mysteries received a strange post card.

The letter from an anonymous person went like this: "Forget Circleville, Ohio. If you come to Ohio, you el sickos will pay." In the end, it was signed, "The Circleville Writer".

Despite the warning, the letter only seemed to have fueled the interest of Unsolved Mysteries, so they dug into what was really in Circleville and found out more than what they bargained for.

More than 4 decades ago, Circleville, Ohio, with a population of only 13,000, was disturbed by a series of letters sent to the homes of some of the residents. The mysterious writer used block letters and it contained personal information about the recipient.

The first letter was sent to Mary Gillispie, a woman working as a school bus driver. The letter was very malicious as it accused her of having an affair to a school official despite the fact that she was married and had children with her husband. The writer also told her that the affair should better stop.

Mary's first reaction was to ignore the letters and hide it from her husband in the fear that it would upset him, but the letters kept on arriving and each one was more threatening than the first. "I know where you live, I've been observing your house and know you have children, this is no joke, please take it serious."

Mary felt helpless, not only were the contents of the letters disturbing, she also had no way of knowing who they came from. Although the letters were postmarked

Columbus, Ohio, there was no return address, and there was no signature.

After two weeks, Ron, Mary's husband, also started receiving letters, the first one read: "Gillispie, you had two weeks and done nothing, make her admit the truth and inform the school board." The sender also cautioned Ron that if he didn't do as he was told, he would broadcast the affair in TV shows and posters.

By this time, the rumor mill about Mary's affair had already started and the family became the center of gossip stage. Unable to bear the pressure, Ron and Mary confided to three people: Ron's sister, her husband, Paul Freshour, and Paul's sister. Mary already had an inkling on who the sender was, but without proof, they couldn't just accuse him of anything, so they developed a plan.

According to Paul, they sent their suspect several letters, nothing violent; just that they knew it was him. "We thought we'd scare the guy," Paul said.

For a while, their plan worked: the letters stopped arriving, but on August 19, 1977, Ron received a phone call. No one knew who the caller was, but it seemed to have confirmed their suspicion about their suspect. Ron became angry that he took his gun and told his children that he was going to confront the letter sender.

He left in his red pickup but on the way to his destination (which was still unknown), he lost control of the vehicle, hit a tree, and was killed.

Martin Yant, a local journalist, found Ron's death to be very suspicious. First was because Ron didn't appear to be drunk when he left the house, but he got into an accident in an area he knew by heart. Second, the gun he'd been carrying was fired once, so somewhere between riding the pickup and hitting the tree, he tried to shoot someone, who and why?

Then a surprising test result showed up: Ron had .16 % of alcohol in his blood! It was very suspicious not just for his children who didn't see him leave the house drunk, but also to the people who knew him who insisted that he was not a heavy drinker, .16 was 1 ½ times more than the legal limit.

Paul Freshour, Ron's brother-in-law, talked to the sheriff, and at first, he appeared to have agreed that there was foul play. But after some time, he changed his attitude and told Paul that the suspect passed the polygraph test, and that there was no foul play-- Ron's death was just an accident.

After Ron passed away, a lot of things took place, one of which was the confession from both Mary and the schools superintendent that they were indeed having an affair. However, they stated that their relationship only started after the letters started arriving.

Some letters were also sent to residents, saying that the sheriff was "covering up" what really happened to Ron, although it wasn't clear if the letters also came from the Circleville Writer, especially since if the sheriff was really involved in a conspiracy, then he was protecting Ron's killer, who could well be the anonymous writer.

Mary continued working as a school bus driver, but the letters didn't stop harassing her family. One time, while driving, she saw a sign intent on ruining her name. In her frustration, she ripped the sign down, but to her surprise, a small box was behind it.

Curious, Mary took the box with her to the bus. When she opened it, there was a small pistol with a string attached to it-- from there she realized that it was booby trap intent on firing the gun at her to get her killed.

Of course, she brought it to the police and the authorities noticed that the serial number was intentionally scratched, probably to protect the identity of the owner. They then took it to the laboratory in the hope that they could still discover the serial number-- they weren't disappointed, but the finding was shocking: the gun belonged to Paul Freshour, who recently just broke up with Ron's sister.

Paul admitted to the fact that the pistol belonged to him, but he reiterated that it had been too long since he'd last seen it. He didn't bother checking it and never once thought it to be missing. "I didn't know what happened, and it's the truth," Paul said. But since the evidence was setting him up, Sheriff Radcliff asked Paul to take a handwriting test.

On February 25, 1983, the sheriff took some actual letters from the Circleville Writer and asked Paul to write them "as close to the letters as he could". Knowing in himself that he was innocent, Paul conceded.

From there, things started to go downhill for Paul. The sheriff searched his garage and took whatever things he deemed as evidence and presented them to court. He also announced that it was Paul's writing found on the booby trap that Mary discovered, Paul was charged with attempted murder, with a cash bond of $50,000.

From an outsider's point of view, it was clear that Paul was framed. First, the handwriting test was not valid because that's not how one should conduct the test. "If they're copying from a letter, then they're going to try to emulate the style." Taking this into consideration, the court didn't charge Paul for the letters, but why did they still use it as strong evidence against him?

More than that, how could the sheriff be so sure that it was his writing found on the sign near the booby trap? During the trial, a handwriting expert offered his opinion that the Circleville Writer was really Paul, and then Paul's boss attested that he was not at work on the day Mary found the trap. In the end, Paul was sentenced to serve time in prison from 7 to 25 years for an attempted murder case.

With Paul in prison, the people of Ohio thought that the letters would stop-- they didn't. In fact, they kept on coming, so Sheriff Radcliff instructed the police to put Paul in solitary confinement. Still, the letters persisted.

It was becoming clear that Paul was not the writer since all the letters were postmarked in Columbus, but he was detained in Lima. However, this was not enough for the court to release Paul, he still served time for 7 years, and after that, his parole request was denied.

Ironically, the decision was based from the fact that the letters kept on coming! They consciously chose to be blind on this, even when Paul himself received a letter in prison, mocking him because he was set up. "Now, when are you going to believe that you aren't going to get out of there?", the letter said.

Was there no evidence that it was a set up?

Martin Yant said there was. He reviewed Sheriff Radcliff's file and noticed that there was information not mentioned during the trial. Apparently, Mary told the Sheriff that a fellow bus driver spoke with her about a yellow El Camino car that she saw in the area where the booby trap was set up.

Apparently, the bus driver was trudging the same route 20 minutes before Mary arrived there. She also reported on seeing a "large man with sandy hair" who pretended to go to the bathroom when he noticed that someone saw him. The description didn't match Paul at all. Why didn't the police follow this lead?

After 10 years of being in prison, Paul was finally released, and he maintained his innocence. He wanted trusted authorities to look at the case again, especially Ron's death because he truly believed it to be murder.

What do you think about this case? It's still unsolved to this day, so if you ever feel the need to crack it, here are some things you can ponder on:

Could it be Mary and/or the schools superintendent who killed Ron? After all, his death would mean freedom for them to continue their relationship. Don't you think it was a little odd for them to admit that they were having an affair, but stating that it started after the letters kept on coming? Could they also be the one to set up Paul? After all, when Mary found the sign, the pistol didn't fire at all.

Did someone intoxicate Ron before his death? His children attested that he wasn't drunk when he left, and yet lab test revealed he was driving under the influence of alcohol. It seemed like he also knew exactly where he was going, so whoever talked to him on the phone was probably a person he knew well.

Why did the police announce his death to be accident when his gun was fired?

And most importantly, who was the Circleville Writer, and why was he/she so invested in Mary's affair? Could it be the superintendent's wife? Some mystery enthusiasts believe so.

From 1970's to 1990's these letters kept on coming, but it all suddenly stopped. The Circleville Writer and Ron's killer (if it was truly a murder), however, could still be at large.

Chapter 4:

When on Highway 16

Canada's Highway 16 was renamed as the Highway of Tears after many women disappeared in the area. The 800-mile stretch of road from Prince George to Prince Rupert in British Columbia literally became the downfall of 43 women in 3 decades time.

May 27, 2011 was supposed to be a happy day in Maddison Scott's life. She and her friends attended a birthday party and after that, they planned on camping out. Wise choice, some would say, because the area was a beautiful spot and it was close to the town.

Dawn Scott, Maddy's mother, tried to call her on her cellphone the next day, but it went straight to voice-mail. She didn't worry though; the area had a lake and cellphone signal there was often spotty. She trusted her daughter to call them in case something bad came up, Maddy never called but it didn't mean nothing bad happened either.

For her parents, it seemed so wrong for Maddy not to call when it was Sunday, so Dawn, together with her husband

and Maddy's father, Eldon, drove to Hogsback Lake where the camping took place. Their home in Vanderhoof was along the stretch of Highway 16 and it was only 15 minutes away from the supposed campsite.

When they got there, Maddy's tent and truck were present, but she was nowhere to be found. Dawn and Eldon's worries grew: the road was notorious for "taking" women and never returning them back. Since 1969, a lot of girls went missing on Highway 16, and the loving parents didn't want Maddy to be included in the figures.

But she was.

When her parents saw her pickup, her backpack and purse were inside, but her phone was missing. From worry, the parent's began to feel panic. They knew their daughter wouldn't go anywhere without her purse, and other personal belongings. The Royal Canadian Mounted Police arrived at the scene to investigate-- their conclusion was straightforward, Maddy was abducted.

"Something happened to Maddy, she didn't get taken by flying saucer. Somebody knew something," said Sgt. Ken Floyd. As part of the protocol, Sgt. Floyd together with Constable Tom Wamsteeker, investigated those who were closely related to Maddy.

They learned that she was a well-liked person in the

community, and that she loved outdoors, hence her excitement for the May 27 camping. She was also close to her brother, Ben and sister, Georgia. Right after graduating high school, she worked with her father in the logging business.

They also interviewed Maddy's closest friends, Amanda Fitzpatrick and Jasmine Klassen, according to them, Maddy "always shared" and would often "take charge" whenever ideas from the group were divided.

Unfortunately, Amanda and Jasmine didn't go camping with Maddy so the police had to interview all the other 50 attendees. It was clear, however, that they still didn't found anyone who had a grudge on the 20-year old girl.

But there was an interesting and creepy twist: during the interview of the attendees, the RMCP found out that all of Maddy's friends didn't camp out-- they packed up and went home, very far from the original idea that they would stay the night out there.

That meant Maddy was left in the lake, all alone, even Jordy Bolduc, Maddy's best friend, who had promised that she would stay with her, left the lake.

According to Constable Wasmteeker, what Maddy knew was that they were all camping, if not all, then most of them. Her mother was devastated, "It's just so wrong."

When Jordy was asked, she admitted that the police interrogated her and asked her several times if she was the culprit, if she had killed Maddy.

She also experienced a lot of backlash from people, accusing her of being stupid and horrible. The explanation as to why and how she left would be discussed later.

Eldon and Dawn, heartbroken from the disappearance of their daughter and frustrated from the lack of progress, started to perform their own investigation. They arranged the basement of their home to serve as their office because they had to track a lot of things, like all of those who went to the camp, who they went with, when they left, and who they left with.

They also retraced Maddy's activities on that day, until they arrived at a bit of security footage showing Maddy while she was visiting a liquor store and buying snacks. They suspected that it was only a matter of hours after the footage was taken before Maddy would vanish.

In the Scott's basement, a board was created, and there was a section there labelled **Questions**. The first questions that Eldon and Dawn had was, why did everyone leave the camp, and why did they leave Maddy alone? So here came the interview with Jordy.

According to her, it was just supposed to be a small party, but since it was broadcast on Facebook, a lot of people attended. Most of the people who first came were known to them, but as the party went on, and many still arrived, the guests became total strangers. At one point during the party, a fight happened and Jordy was caught in the middle of it, resulting in an injury.

Her boyfriend carried her to his truck and then after some time, they decided to leave. They told Maddy of their decision, but Maddy begged her to stay. Since Jordy lost interest in the party which was clearly becoming more intense than they expected it to be, she insisted on going home and asked Maddy to come with them.

Maddy refused and said that she wanted to stay behind with her tent. So at around 1:00 in the morning, Jordy left with her boyfriend, but the next day, while feeling guilty for leaving Maddy behind, she went to the lake to at least help her pack up, but Maddy wasn't there. She checked her pickup and her tent, but there was still no sign of Maddy. She also reported that the tent was a mess, with the door flaps open and the blankets pushed to the side.

Her rings were also found on the ground, as well as her earrings. Since she knew her friend didn't like taking off her rings, she wondered immediately where Maddy was. But she was as clueless as everyone else.

As expected, Jordy became one of the suspects, because she was one of the few people whom Maddy had a conversation with before she went missing. In a period of three months, she took two polygraph tests, which she both passed. In the end, Constable Wamsteeker admitted that Jordy was removed from the suspects list.

From Jordy, the police centered their investigation to a logger, Fribjon "Frib" Bjornson. According to reports, he had been telling people that he knew what happened to Maddy and rumors had it that the two were seeing each other. When informed with this, Jordy couldn't help but be shocked.

Frib, a father of two children, was a known troublemaker who got himself involved in drugs, a fact which the police themselves confirmed. Frib's mother, however, insisted that his son was turning away from his troubled past life.

With the news of Maddy's disappearance and her involvement with Frib, people started spouting unconfirmed reports on how Frib owed money to some drug dealers and that Maddy was taken as revenge against him. Despite the fact that it was unconfirmed, the police didn't ignore the rumors.

They went to Frib, who was by then already considered a suspect, and asked him to undergo a lie detector test, which he passed. Now all could have been over since the police cleared him (mainly due to passing the polygraph test), but Frib disappeared after just two days.

And then, two weeks later, the police found his severed head. 4 people had been arrested with regards to Frib's murder, but unfortunately, his death wasn't connected to Maddy's disappearance.

Dawn and Eldon are still hopeful to find their daughter alive up to this day. They even issued $100,000 reward money for anyone who had information regarding Maddy's disappearance.

Hope for Maddy is still strong, especially if it wasn't a work of a serial killer, but 15 year old Loren Leslie was robbed of luck: she was murdered.

Midnight of November 27, 2010 (almost 7 months before Maddy disappeared), Doug Leslie, Loren's father, received a strange call. The caller was a policemen, and he was inquiring if Loren was at home, Doug was instantly on alert, so he asked what was happening.

The caller replied that if Loren was home, it would be strange because someone was using her ID. "What do you mean someone's using her ID?" Doug asked, the policemen only replied that they had found Loren's ID in a vehicle.

Brody Clayton

He made the police promise to call him back in case anything about Loren turned up, but when he they didn't and he still couldn't get hold of his daughter, he went on a drive to the notorious Highway of Tears.

Unknown to him, hours before his drive in search for Loren, an RMCP constable stopped a black pickup truck which suddenly emerged from the woods. The constable didn't quite like how the 20 year old man inside the pickup was acting, so he kept him while asking another officer to check the area where he came from.

They expected to see an elk, or maybe a moose, because the man might have been a poacher, but instead, they found the body of 15 year old Loren Leslie.

As if he knew his daughter had been found, Doug reached the area at that same moment. Since it was his intention to really find the policemen, he went near the scene and saw that one of the officers was shocked. He told them who he was and what his intentions were, but the police only responded that they were investigating a homicide case.

Doug knew that it was his daughter they were investigating, but since he was a father, he still clung to that small hope that it wasn't Loren, especially when they told him that they couldn't identify the victim because her face was badly beaten.

Bravely, Doug asked them to look at the wrist and see if the victim had a unique tattoo which says "Grip Fast". The warden checked and Doug's worst fears came to life: the victim had that tattoo, it really was Loren.

During interviews, Doug was emotional while recalling that moment. He showed his wrist because he also had the same tattoo, which was a family motto meaning "Hang tight."

Loren was reportedly beaten using a pipe wrench and was also sexually assaulted on top of having her throat slit. The police asked Doug if he knew anyone who could do such a thing to his daughter, but he only replied that whoever he was, he wasn't human.

Was Cody Legebokoff, the 20 year old man whose black pickup was found in the woods, the killer? At the time of Loren's death, the police only suspected him, after all, he was found at the same time they discovered her body. He was apparently familiar with the 15 year old through the internet because like him, Loren too was an avid social media user.

The problem was, Cody was a well-liked boy. He was a high school graduate with a stable job in a Ford dealership company, on top of that, he lived in a house with three girl room-mates, all of whom had nothing bad to tell about him.

George Anatole, a friend of Cody's, couldn't believe it when he heard that Cody was being suspected of Loren's murder. "He was popular, he got along with everybody, he was fun."

The RMCP didn't give the details, but a year after Loren's murder, they announced Cody as the killer. They had also pointed him as the murderer of three other girls, the only statement they provided was that Cody started killing at the age of 19, very young for a serial killer. Was Cody also responsible for Maddy Scott's disappearance?

No. According to the police, Cody was already in custody when Maddy went missing. On top of that, after investigating, the RMCP concluded that no one who attended the camping party was responsible for Maddy's vanishing.

Was the mystery of the Highway of Tears' murders and disappearances solved? Another no. They did however, find one man who could be responsible for more than 20 murders, not just on Highway 16, but all throughout Canada.

This was thanks to the new technology which they used to match a man's DNA to that found on Colleen McMillen, another Highway 16 victim in 1974. Bobby Fowler was the said murderer, but since he was a known criminal, he was already in prison when the police learned of his connection to the Highway 16 murders, and in 2006, he was already dead.

For the RMCP, even though Bobby wasn't punished for those crimes, it was still a major victory. Hopefully, something new will also come up for Maddy and the other victims who were taken by the Highway of Tears.

Chapter 5:
The Cannibal of Ziebice

In the small town of Ziebice, Poland – then Munsterberg, Silesia – Karl Denke ran a rooming house for vagabonds and homeless people, giving them shelter from the elements and allowing them to rest their weary souls. He was largely liked and respected by the community, acted as the organ-blower for his local church and was often called 'Papa' by his tenants.

In Decemeber of the year 1924, one of the good hotel owner's tenants, a coachman who went by the name of Gabriel, was going about his business when he heard a cry for help from Denke's home.

He became worried that his landlord may have been injured or hurt and rushed down to see what happened, only to find a young man, staggering and stumbling down the hallway, crimson drops of blood dripping down the side of his face. His scalp was cut open and he was shaking, dizzy from the head wound.

Before he succumbed to unconsciousness, the young man blurted out that 'Papa Denke' attacked him with an axe. Shocked and upset, Gabriel had no choice but to call the police, who arrested him and took him into custody.

Investigations were conducted, digging into the life of the man who had been a quiet presence in the community. And then came out the truth – Karl Denke, respected local, was a serial killer who had murdered – and probably eaten – close to 40 victims, all of whom were vagabonds and homeless travellers, who would not be missed if they vanished.

Born on the 10th of August in the year 1870, Karl Denke was, perhaps, one of the most unremarkable men to have ever lived. He did not have a spectacular childhood with any bitter memories; he was apparently a dull, somewhat retarded child, who did not even complete school.

He took on a post as a gardener's apprentice at the young age of 12; his family was quite well off financially, so he went through little to no hardships as a young boy. Once his father passed away, his brother took over their family farm, while Denke himself received money enough to buy some farm land a little ways away.

However, his career as a farmer was not very successful,

and he ended selling it and fighting the recession period of the economy until he settled down with the rooming house that would later house many of his victims.

Denke's history as a murderer is one that is shrouded in mystery; the man himself was a coward, or so it seems. The night of his arrest, he killed himself in his cell, unwilling to stand trial for all his crimes. What we do know about his career as a serial killer, is knowledge that comes mostly from the police investigations, a journal which he had kept with detailed victim accounts and research published by Lucyna Bialy, who looked into him as part of her project on the German press.

Since it is entirely second hand information, we cannot be too sure of his motives or reasons for his action, only that he did kill so many and even went as far as to partake of their flesh.

It is understandable that the police initially refused to believe the young man who accused 'Papa Denke' of such a heinous act. Denke was a respected man of the community, while the young chap – Vincenz Oliver – was only a vagabond. Add to that the strong ties that small communities have for one another and it is no surprise that the police were absolutely astonished and disbelieving of the story.

But evidence could not lie, and evidence stated that Oliver was attacked with a heavy cutting tool. A doctor confirmed his story, and the police had little choice in arresting Denke as protocol demanded. Denke himself confessed to having attacked Oliver, but he claimed that he did not know who the vagabond was, pretending that he was a burglar trying to rob his property.

Perhaps he had known even then that his story was flimsy at best, and that his life as a well-respected citizen was coming to an end. Karl Denke had no intentions of standing trials for his crimes; the next morning, the police found his body within his cell.

He had hung himself to death using a handkerchief.

And when the police raided his house, they found disturbing things – from body parts to strips of human meat, all clearly proving Denke's penchant for murder and gore. The acting head of the Institute of Legal Medicine in Breslau, Friedrich Pietrusky, went so far as to publish a report based on their findings.

The first thing the police saw in their raid of Denke's home were strips of meat and bare bones of human beings. The meat was found in a big, wooden drum, which contained a salt solution that kept the strips – around 15 pieces, with human skin attached – fresh.

Among these pieces, the police found breast parts, parts of a human torso, stomach and shoulders. The largest part, Pietrusky said in his report, was a very clean anus that still had both buttocks attached to it.

Given that the meat was a brownish red in color, and the status of the livor mortis, the doctors concluded that the body was cut apart several hours after death. The problem was that there was no evidence of how the victim was killed; the cuts were made after death, and while there was skin, muscles and other body parts – like the limbs, head and sexual organs – missing, the nature of death or the murder weapon could not really be pinpointed.

Following the barrel, the police then found three pots of cream sauce, which contained meat as much as it did sauce. The meat was still covered with skin and hair and was *"...pink and soft."* Pietrusky claimed that these pieces were cut from the gluteal area – the buttocks – and since one pot contained only half a portion, he assumed that Denke had eaten the rest.

His assumption is logical and makes sense, but there was no evidence to prove it. His conclusion was entirely circumstantial; there were claims that Denke had sold the meat, though this was also never verified. In his report, Pietrusky even mentioned that it was possible for Denke to have offered some of the meat to his vagabond guests – true or not, this is a disturbing image.

There was yet another pot with more human remains in it, which tested positive for human protein, proving the existence of a third victim. The police moved further into the house, already shuddering in horror and disgust at their discoveries.

In the shed, they found another barrel, filled with tendons, muscles and other human parts that had been already cooked. When they took the barrel apart, they found six forearm bones – proof of at least three victims stuffed within that single barrel.

Denke had dug himself a pond many years previously behind his house; what better way to rid himself of extra human remains than dumping it into the water? No one would suspect him, and no one did suspect him, until he messed up and one of his victims escaped him and he was caught.

Needless to say that the police found human remains when they raided the pond as well, particularly the part of a leg separate from all the other remains they had found so far, indicating the incidence of yet another victim.

Apart from the bodies and the remains themselves, the police also found the weapons that had killed these poor men and women. Peitrusky claimed that axes, wood and tree saws, pickaxes, knives and the like were sent to him and his lab for testing – all tested positive for residue of human remains, indicating that they were murder weapons.

'Papa Denke' had been cutting, hacking and killing the vagabonds he took in, promising them home and shelter, instead leading them to their deaths. What is even more surprising than anything else is the utter lack of motive in the case of Karl Denke – most serial killers have had troubled childhoods or traumatic past incidents that triggered their need to take life. Denke, on the other hand, led an easy childhood.

The only indication of mental trauma comes from his schooling, where his teachers thought him dull, unintelligent and stupid. Given that he did not speak until the age of six, it's not surprising that he did not do well in his classes, but still, there was not trauma enough to lead to start killing.

His family were more shocked than anyone else; on

inquiry, they swore that he displayed few signs of aggressive tendencies. He did not showcase the violent temper that must have led him to start butchering people in such a gruesome manner. He kept to himself, though, and attended few family dinners – his brother recalled that he had a massive appetite.

Once, he stated, Karl ate 2 full pounds of meat by himself! He called Denke a glutton, but in essence, a good, if solitary man.

Though he was well respected within his community, his neighbours later reported that he was a suspicious man, whose private life was something they had been wondering at for years. The entire town could hardly believe that one of their own was such a monster, and yet admitted to treating him with suspicion, albeit due to his status as a solitary man.

In a small town, tightly knit community, his sexual indifference was something of a confusing enigma. Despite that, his humble behavior, the occasional contributions to charity and community, all earned him the nickname 'Father Denke' and he was regarded as one of their own.

The evidence found in his home indicates that he had

killed more than 30 people – did he eat all of them? Did he truly sell their meat in the town fairs as so many claim he did? It is a disturbing image – anyone could have bought that meat and taken it back home to feed their families.

Who Denke truly was and why he murdered so many people will remain a true mystery. That the man was a coward is obvious – he took his own life on the night of his arrest, unwilling to face his crimes. His motives and personality hardly fall in line with the general ideologies of serial killers, who tend to be psychopathic in nature more often than not.

Denke, on the other hand, was more rational than psychotic, was not motivated sexually – none of the remains showed signs of sexual assault – and had no real trauma that could have triggered his need to kill.

What seems to have been was simply a man with an extraordinary hunger – literally. Was it that he did not want to harm anybody but his hunger for meat was just too extreme?

From what we know of him, he appears to have been a selfish, retarded man, unable to distinguish right from wrong – was it just that he wanted to find himself good food after failing in school, as a gardening apprentice and as a farmer? Was he simply looking at the vagabonds as potential food, like a butcher would the animals in his care?

We can never truly know.

Chapter 6:
Hunting Children – The Family Business

Murderous tendencies are that dark side of humanity that we would rather not think about, that we would prefer to deny exists. But when these tendencies display themselves horrifically and ruin more lives than we can count, we have no choice but to sit up and take action, if only to protect the innocents.

That is what happened in the case of Renuka Shinde, her sister and her mother – the three made hunting people and killing them their family business.

What is most disturbing about these women is that they wore the faces of ordinary people like you and me. If you searched for images of them on Google, you would find nothing striking about Renuka Shinde, Seema Mohan Gavit or their mother Anjanabaai. Three women from Maharashtra, India, destroyed countless lives, murdering innocent children between the ages of 5-9 by bashing their heads repeatedly against hard surfaces.

Their horrific tale began with their mother, Anjanabaai, who raised them in the life of a petty crime. Seema and Renuka, along with the latter's husband, Kiran Shinde, lived out their lives as petty thieves, stealing and making off with what they could from the local small shops and vendors.

On one such instance, Renuka was caught pick-pocketing at the Chatursinghi temple in Pune. At the time, she had her little son, Ashish, with her, and it didn't take her long to convince the crowd gathered there that a mother with a toddler in hand would hardly be stealing. The crowd finally let her go, and it was then that the seeds of such perversion took root.

When Renuka returned to her criminal family and narrated the incident, they all realized what a perfect diversion the child made. Nobody would suspect an innocent mother with a child of being a criminal; in the worst case scenario that someone did, then they could use the child as a distraction to make their own hurried getaway.

Renuka, her mother and her sister were already hunted by the police for their petty crimes, which meant that kidnapping young toddlers was the perfect cover they needed to continue their family business in a safe manner.

And thus began the kidnappings. Little boys and girls between the ages of 5-9 were snatched off the roads and brought into their gang, forced to work for them. If they refused to do so, or cried and made a fuss – as toddlers are generally prone to doing – then they were killed right away, usually by bashing their heads repeatedly against a wall or an electricity pole.

Renuka and Seema were half-sisters; the former's father was Anjanabaai's second husband, Mohan, who had left his wife when he sensed something wrong with her. He married another woman and raised a family with her instead – Anjanabaai wanted revenge.

Hell truly hath no fury like a woman scorned, and in this case, that meant a death sentence for Mohan's elder daughter from his second marriage. Renuka, abandoned by her father, began her killing spree by murdering her half-sister.

And then, they were off. Railway stations, bus stops, temples, local fairs – any grounds where there was a large gathering of people, they stalked in search of innocent victims. Their getaway driver was Renuka's husband,

Kiran Shinde, who would later testify against them when they were caught. But for now, he was well and firmly entrenched in their plots.

Their victims were children of the poor families – families who couldn't afford to go to the police, whose kids would not be missed by anyone other than their parents. It was only later that lawyers lamented the fact that the police did not take these complaints seriously – too many lives were lost because of their indifference to the lower sections of society.

The first child whose life was sacrificed to the mad women's plots was a one-year old baby by the name of Santosh. His mother was a beggar woman, and they took him off the streets, using him as a distraction. As one sister held the baby and kept the crowd occupied, the other quietly went around and would start stealing wallets, jewellery and anything worth taking from the crowd.

And when she got caught, the baby was thrown to the ground, where – needless to say – he started crying, keeping the crowd's attention on him until they could get away. This, in fact, became their modus operandi, and it wasn't just Santosh who was given this treatment.

And if the children became a burden or a nuisance, they were simply murdered, since the mother and sisters were hardly interested in raising them. Young Santosh was hurled to the ground on one of their crimes; they had no medication to soothe his injuries, and without it, they festered. A baby could hardly speak its pain out loud – little wonder that Santosh kept crying from the ache of his injuries.

Instead of soothing him or at least leaving him on the road for some good soul to find, Anjanabaai repeatedly bashed his head against an iron rod in an effort to shut him up. And he did shut up – forever. The sisters watched their mother murder the baby boy while they were munching on snacks.

In this manner, they continued on for months on end, kidnapping and killing innocent children to feed their own perverse tastes. Little Swapnil – barely seven months old and just beginning to walk – lost his life to Seema's hands. She threw him against a wall when she got irritated by his constant crying. Another two year old boy was hung up and had his head slammed against a wall repeatedly.

Perhaps the most disturbing of all was how cool and calm

they were about the whole idea. They chopped up the body of one child, throwing the pieces into a gunny bag to dispose of later. They took the bag with them into the movie theatre and sat down to relax with a plate of *bhel puri*, while the bag with the murdered child lay at their feet.

And so, the mother and sisters reined terror for over six years, between 1990-96. The exact number of children they kidnapped and killed is unknown – the police believe they murdered 9 of the 13 children that they snatched off the streets.

The sisters were finally caught when they went to kidnap Mohan's second daughter as well. Fortunately, his wife had filed a complaint against them when her first child went missing, and this time, the police caught them without hitches. Their mother was also brought in and together, the trio were questioned.

It didn't take long for the police to raid their haunts and find evidence of what appeared to be more than just kidnappings. What they uncovered, though, was horrific enough that the case was quickly handed over to the Criminal Investigation Department (CID) of the government.

As the investigation took place, the police narrowed in on Kiran Shinde, who had acted in the capacity of a getaway driver for his wife and her accomplices. Whether he himself killed any of the victims is unclear; all we know is that he turned and confessed all the details to the police. The women, however, remained impassive in the faces of the charges being leveled against them – they flatly denied all accusations and insisted that they were being framed.

The mother, Anjanabaai, would not stand to face justice for her crimes – she died during the course of the trial itself. But the sisters would face justice- the High Court of Maharashtra found them guilty of five accounts of murder.

It was only five that the prosecution could prove, despite the 9 murders they were accused of, not to mention the many kidnappings. In any case, justice would not be denied, and justice demanded that they be thrown in Yerwada Jail in Pune while their sentence was being decided.

What is even more disturbing, perhaps, is the stubborn tenacity with which the sisters clung to their claims of innocence. *"....they want to know about the status of their mercy petition...*" said a jail official. When the Supreme Court's verdict arrived, the sisters were separated and Renuka was moved to the Nagpur jail, where an advocate, Swati Saroday, was called to work with her in order to rehabilitate her four children to normal society.

Saroday recalls that the woman was irritable and tetchy, going on frequent hunger strikes if her demands were not met. She called for her sister constantly, as well as her children, fretting about them constantly.

That she would worry so much over the fate of her own children while ruthlessly murdering and maiming other innocent babies is disturbing and worrying. Finally, Reunka was transferred back to the Yerwada jail, though lodged in a separate cell from her sister.

Her children were initially regular visitors, but the visits tapered off as her eldest son began to grow up. When he turned 18, he took custody of his siblings and left the remand home, vanishing from the public eye.

The verdict finally arrived much later. The Supreme Court declared that the women were of a 'depraved mind', killing without compulsion or reason, and thereby sentenced them to death. And depraved mind was truly the fact here – the sisters were more concerned with why Renuka's inmate received more hot water during her illness than they were of their own fate or the fates of the children they had murdered.

They believed in their innocence, and that, perhaps, more than anything, is horrifying.

Chapter 7:
The High Priestess of Blood

Religion and cult sacrifices have taken more lives than we could possibly account for. Magdalena Solis, known as the *'High Priestess of Blood'*, was a Mexican cult killer, who believed herself to be the reincarnated form of an ancient goddess. Like most serial killers, she had her own psychotic breaks, rising from a life of poverty and disparity.

Magdalena Solis is one of the very few documented cases of a female serial killer who was also into sexual perversions. She was reported to be one of the few female sex offenders, who organized and conducted gory, bloody murders that were sexual in nature.

Mad though she may have been, she was also quite cunning in her plans, and she managed to raise an entire cult around herself, sitting on a throne – literally – as their goddess.

Solis was born into a poor family, and as with most girls in her situation, she ended up working as a prostitute from a very young age. What is even more disturbing is the fact that her own brother acted as her pimp, spending his days trying to find a wealthy man to bed his sister for the night and pay her handsomely for it. Eleazar Solis continued in this manner for years, until the Hernandez brothers found them in the year 1963.

To digress a little, let me tell you the story of Santos and Cayetano Hernandez, without whom Solis's career as goddess/murderess would not have been possible. Santos and Cayetano were simply two petty criminals operating close to a small town called Yerba Buena in northern Mexico.

They came up with what they believed was a brilliant plan to cheat the people of this town out of their money – they claimed themselves to be prophets and priests of the *"...powerful and exiled Inca gods"*.

Given that the community was pretty secluded from the rest of the world, mostly illiterate and suffering from extreme poverty, it was not surprising that they accepted the brothers' utterly ridiculous claims almost immediately. The Hernandez boys were quite ignorant themselves; they had no idea that the 'Inca gods' were part of the mythology that belonged to pre-Hispanic Peru, not Mexico. Despite that, the community, which was not even 100 in number, accepted their claims and bowed down to them.

Santos and Cayetano told them that in return for worship and tribute, the Inca Gods would bring them gold and treasure. There were numerous mountains in the region, each of which had their own caves, and the boys used these to cover their stories, claiming that the treasures were hidden here, and the gods would reveal them when they were satisfied.

Worse still, to convince those who did not believe them, they claimed that the gods would claim authority over the area – their former kingdom – and then take the unbelievers into their own hands, punishing them as they saw fit.

The inhabitants of Yerba Buena, poor and illiterate and desperate for some relief from the daily toil that was their lives, accepted the Hernandez brothers' claims. They gave in to their demands and formed a religious sect, bowing their heads to the would-be deities. And the two petty criminals took full advantage.

They demanded tributes in the form of monetary and

sexual taxes, calling on both men and women to participate in their rituals. They became sexual slaveholders and conducted regular orgies, where they forced the poor villagers to partake of narcotics and perform disturbing sexual acts.

For some time, the cult ran in this manner, adhering to every whim and fancy of the 'high priests', who never tired of running their sect religiously. But soon, the villagers grew suspicious – none of the promised gold or treasure appeared, despite giving in to every single one of the Hernandez brothers' demands. They wanted the promised goods and began to demand the truth from the brothers.

Now Santos and Cayetano had no choice but to either come clean or take their charade a step further – needless to say, they took the latter option. They devised yet another plan; they reached out to their criminal contacts and tried to find someone to help them. They left the village and headed to Monterrey, where they began to look for prostitutes who would consent to be a part of their farce.

Enter Magdalena and her brother, both of whom were running dry in the prostitution business. When they saw the opportunity the brothers presented, they jumped at the chance and agreed immediately to be part of the sect, returning to Yerba Buena with Santos and Cayetano.

The brothers then devised her entry into the sect – they called for a ritual with all the cult members present, and then using the cheap trick of a smokescreen, presented Magdalena Solis as their goddess.

And then began Solis's career as the powerful goddess who would rain death and destruction down on those who crossed her. Neither the Hernandez brothers nor her own brother had expected that she herself would believe in the illusion they were perpetrating. Magdalena's mind broke – she accepted her role as reincarnated goddess and fulfilled all her repressed, disturbing sexual and murderous fantasies through her new calling.

When she joined the sect, she developed a severe theological psychosis. She became the proverbial religious fanatic, suffering from delusions of grandeur and religion; her sexually perverse tastes found the outlet that not even being a prostitute had given her.

From drinking the blood of her victims to practising incest and paedophilia, she had a way to justify all her perversions, proclaiming them to be the demands of the goddess that she had once been and now once again was.

It didn't take too long for her to take complete control of the sect itself. Within months, she had them running to fulfil her every demand, bidding her brother and the Hernandez boys to continue acting in their posts as her high priests.

They organized disturbing rituals, orgies and the like, where drugs continued to be used. But now along with drugs and sex, there were also other practices, of a more violent nature, like beatings and whippings.

By this time, two of the members had grown tired of the constant sexual and physical abuse – they wanted to leave the cult. When they admitted to this, they were brought in front of Magdalena, in all her 'goddess' glory; the entire cult was also called to witness their trial to set an example of them. The high priests accused them of treason and called for their deaths.

The two were killed publicly, in front of the rest of their tribesmen, who now began to tremble in fear and agreed to do whatever was asked of them.

These two murders triggered Magdalena's lust for blood;

her crimes escalated, becoming more and more perverse, more and more violent and disturbing. Up until now, she had orgies, whippings and beatings – now she wanted people to be sacrificed in her name. She was a true goddess, an ancient power of magic and majesty, and the mere mortals feared and sacrificed themselves to please her. With that thought in mind, she slowly came up with a new ritual that would keep these victims bound to her for all eternity.

This blood ritual was disturbing and frightening – she called for a victim (always one rebellious or dissenting member of the cult who had crossed her in some manner or the other) to be brought before the entire sect, which would assemble on her bidding. Then, the dissenting member would be tortured by the entire sect together – anyone who refused to do so would join the victim too.

First they would be beaten brutally, and then burnt and branded. Following this, they would be cut and maimed, body parts removed slowly and brutally. Finally, the ritual would conclude with bloodletting, the victim bleeding out to death. The blood itself, as it leaked out from the dying man or woman, was to be collected in a goblet, and then mixed with chicken blood.

The ritual also made use of animal blood and the narcotics that the Hernandez brothers still supplied; marijuana, peyote, chicken blood and the human blood made for a heady combination that left Magdalena delusional and shaking in ecstasy. She would drink from the chalice that contained this disturbing concoction, her entire countenance emanating delight in the pain and suffering of her victims.

She would then offer the drink to her brother, Eleazar Solis, who would drink it as well. After him, the Hernandez brothers were required to partake of the mixture – Santos and Cayetano could hardly refuse, given that Solis's presence in the cult was their fault in the first place.

Finally, each of the cult members was required to take part in the drinking as well. Magdalena claimed that those who did drink it would receive special, supernatural powers from the goddess herself, who, pleased with their efforts, would be looking to reward them richly.

What was even more disturbing was that Magdalena was far more intelligent and cunning than the two brothers. She knew enough to quote from Aztec mythology; she told the cult members that "...*blood was the only decent food for the gods, through which they preserved their immortality."* She knew just how to play into the fears and hopes of the poor villagers.

Perhaps the most disturbing fact of all is that she herself *believed* in what she was saying – she believed herself to be the goddess, whose immortality would remain intact from the partaking of her victims" blood.

She claimed that she was the reincarnation of the Aztec goddess Coatlicue. To give a little background information on this deity – Coatlicue was believed to have been the Aztec goddess who gave birth to the sun, moon and the stars. She was taken to be the primordial earth goddess, who wore a skirt of snakes. The goddess's terrible fury and power are usually emphasized upon; this stems from the belief that the Earth, while being a loving mother, is also an insatiable monster that consumes everything that is alive on it. She is, literally, the devouring mother, in whom there exists the grave as well as the womb.

While scholars may appreciate the dichotomy and ponder over the dual nature of the cosmos that this ancient Aztec myth presents to them, Magdalena Solis used it to bind her cult to her. She was, in essence, the devouring mother – she would protect and look after them, provided they did her every bidding. Otherwise, they would be fed to the grave within her; she would sacrifice them, as was well within her rights as their goddess.

No ridiculous story can work without a grain of truth to it; Magdalena's story was no different. It worked like a charm, and the villagers, trembling in terror, gave in to her, following her every whim and command. For the next six weeks, Magdalena reined fire and anger down upon them, killing 4 more villagers in this manner.

The blood ritual became an almost daily practice and she sat and watched the villagers butcher one another in an effort to please their goddess. The orgies and the sexual abuse continued, but they were now accompanied by the blood ritual. By the time her killing spree drew to a close, she had taken to having the victims' hearts dissected in their chests – while they were still alive.

It was only in May of the year 1963, when a young boy of 14 years, Sebastian Guerrero, caught them in the act. The village of Yerba Buena may have been isolated, but it was only at the coming of the Hernandez brothers that they were completely cut off from the outside world.

Guerrero was a local resident of the area and he wandered

into the caves where the Solis sect was conducting their rites. The boy was a curious lad; the bright lights and the sounds from the caves were intriguing, and like any teenager, he went exploring. He hid behind a rock and watched the entire village butcher and slaughter an unknown victim, draining him of his blood and then drinking it.

Needless to say, the boy was traumatized. Terrified, he raced from the caves and continued to run. For over twenty-five kilometres he ran, his mind throwing up the disturbing images over and over again, his entire form shaking with fear and horror.

Out of Yerba Buena and into the nearby town of Villa Gran, he ran, making straight for the police station. His body trembled with exhaustion and he was in shock; the only things he could say were garbled sentences about a group of killers who *"...prey on ecstasy... gluttonously drinking human blood..."*

It goes without saying that the police officers laughed at the poor boy. They could hardly believe what they were hearing – a bunch of people murdering and drinking the blood of the innocent? Given that the story came out of the mouth of an exhausted teenager, they were less inclined to believe him than ever before, dismissing it as the claims of a disturbed or drug-using boy.

Still, his mad ramblings were enough to warrant sending him home with an officer – they had no idea they would never again see either the boy or the officer.

Investigator Luis Martinez was not convinced, per se, but he was curious as to what the boy was claiming to be the truth. As he took him home, he apparently agreed to check out the site Guerrero had run from, presumably only to prove to the boy that he was imagining things. What he could not have expected was that they would be captured and sacrificed to the goddess Magdalena Solis.

Now that one of their own had vanished, the police had no choice but to sit up and take notice. They began to discuss the possibility of a satanic cult and on the 31st of May; the police – along with the army, whom they had called for backup – deployed a team to check out the site. Eleazar and Magdalena Solis were taken into custody – they were at the time in a farm in Yerba Buena, dosing themselves with marijuana.

What was worse was that the police were unable to save many of the villagers. One would think that police intervention in such a case would at least prevent further death – the opposite happened.

The villagers, who had firmly internalized Magdalena's lies, were terrified of the retribution the goddess would reign down upon them if they went free. They barricaded themselves within the caves and refused to come out, leading to a shootout between them and the police, who had no choice but to lure them out with bullets.

Those who did come out were arrested and sentenced to 30 years of prison on the charges of murder in the form of 'group murder or lynching'. Given their poor conditions, illiteracy and bare knowledge of the world, it isn't surprising that many refused to even speak of the horrors they faced for decades after the end of the cult.

In a sight of divine justice, however, Santos and Cayetano, who had begun the whole farce, faced punishment then and there. Santos was killed in the shootout, but Cayetano was murdered by one of his own cult members. Jesus Rubio had wanted to be a high priest himself, and when refused, became furious. He took advantage of the confusion caused by the police and had the second Hernandez brother assassinated.

Having emptied the caves of the sect, the police began their investigations.

What they found was horrific – they saw carved up bodies, dismembered figures of victims who had no chance of escape. Among them, they also found the remains of Guerrero and Martinez, both of whom had been ritually sacrificed to the goddess. Close to six bodies were found, indicating the existence of at least six victims.

The Solis siblings, however, were charged with the murders of only two – Guerrero and Martinez. Unfortunately, not enough evidence was found to charge them with the rest and the remaining cult members, still fearing the goddess's wrath, refused to testify against them. The trial was straightforward – both Solis siblings were sentenced to 50 years in prison for the two murders.

In her delusional career as a goddess, Magdalena took the lives of at least 8 people. Some sources say she killed at least 15, but no matter how many she actually killed, one must admit that she ruined the lives of an entire village, sexually, physically and emotionally abusing more of them than any of us can count. She was a madwoman, and in the wake of her madness, an entire community suffered.

Conclusion

For the police, Cold Cases could be considered a failure, but for the families left by the victims, it's heartbreaking. They have to live their lives day in and day out knowing that something didn't add up.

However, one must not lose hope, especially with new technology. Take Sherri Rasmussen's and Colleen McMillen's cases for example-- their loved ones literally waited decades before they got the justice they deserved.

Thank you for purchasing this book, I hope you enjoyed it.

If you liked this book I would love it if you could leave me a review on Amazon! Just search for this title and my name to find it. Thank you so much, it is very much appreciated!

Check Out My Other Books

Below you'll find some of my other popular books that are popular on Amazon and Kindle as well. You can visit my author page on Amazon to see other work done by me. (Brody Clayton).

True Murder Stories

Women Who Kill

Serial Killers

Serial Killers – Volume 2

Cold Cases True Crime

Cold Cases True Crime – Volume 2

Cold Cases True Crime – Volume 3

True Crime

True Crime – Volume 2

True Crime – Volume 3

Serial Killers True Crime

Serial Killers True Crime – Volume 2

Serial Killers True Crime – Volume 3

Serial Killers True Crime – Volume 4

True Crime Stories

You can simply search for these titles on the Amazon website with my name to find them.

Brody Clayton

LIBRARY BUGS BOOKS

Like FREE books?

Would you like them delivered to you every week?

Do you like non-fiction books on a huge range of different topics?

We send out FREE e-books every week so we can share our books with the world!

We have FREE books every week on AMAZON that we send to our email list.

If you want in, then visit the link below to sign up and sit back and wait for new books to be sent straight to your inbox!

It couldn't be simpler!

www.LibraryBugs.com

If you want FREE books delivered straight to your inbox, then visit the link above and soon you'll be receiving a great list of FREE e-books every week!

Enjoy :)

CPSIA information can be obtained
at www.ICGtesting.com
Printed in the USA
LVHW102157120323
741474LV00017B/149